SCIENC

Porpoises in Peril

CAM

KATE

JADA

REGGIE

Written by Gwendolyn Hooks
Illustrated by Tony Forbes

Published by Pearson Education Limited, 80 Strand, London, WC2R 0RL.

www.pearsonschools.co.uk

Text © Pearson Education Limited 2016

Original illustrations © Pearson Education Limited

Illustrated by Tony Forbes

First published in the USA by Pearson Education Inc, 2016

First published in the UK by Pearson Education Ltd, 2017

21 20 19

10 9 8 7 6 5 4 3

British Library Cataloguing in Publication Data

A catalogue record for this book is available from the British Library

ISBN 9780435164560

Acknowledgements

We would like to thank Bangor Central Integrated Primary, NI;
Parkfield Primary School, Manchester; St Matthew's CE Primary,
Stretton; Bishop Henderson CE Primary, Somerset; Bridge Learning
Campus, Bristol; Barton Hill Academy, Devon; Southroyd Primary,
Leeds; St John's CE Primary, Maidstone; Sandling Primary, Maidstone;
Lingham Primary, Wirral; Foxdell Infants, Luton; Pennoweth Primary,
Redruth; Clifton-Upon-Teme Primary, Clifton-Upon-Teme; Broadgreen
Primary, Liverpool for their invaluable help in the development and
trialling of the Bug Club resources.

Printed in the UK by Ashford Colour Press

Chapter 1

Jada sprinted into the headquarters of the Global Environmental Research Agency, known as GERA. She ran up five flights of steps to the training room, where her Science Squad colleagues were waiting for her. They were reading through a fat pile of papers – their new assignment.

"Thank you for joining us," Professor Q said.

"Aw, I lost," said Cam, looking glum.

"Lost what? A rare plant?" asked Jada, pulling a tablet from her backpack. Cam was a botanist and had a greenhouse full of rare plants.

"No, I lost the bet with Kate," said Cam. "I bet that you'd be late for our meeting, and now I have to buy her lunch," Cam sighed. "But speaking of plants, I have a new one that you have to see, it . . ."

"Hold on," said Kate. "If he starts talking about plants, our meeting will last twice as long." Kate's dark eyes sparkled, and Reggie, the fourth member of the squad, chuckled.

The professor pushed the forward button on her wheelchair and glided closer to the others. She moved her long plait from her left shoulder to her right shoulder. That was the signal that she was ready to discuss something important. She looked straight at them and said, "Sick porpoises."

Reggie snapped his pencil in half, and his shoulders tensed. He hated hearing about any animal suffering, whether a wild one or a pet.

Professor Q continued:

Local officials spotted several porpoises near an island off the northern coast of Taiwan, behaving strangely. The porpoises have been losing weight quickly, and the officials believe that something or someone has contaminated their food supply.

There is a risk that the porpoise population will decline, and that eventually all the porpoises will die, so the officials have asked for our help. You know how important it is to keep the proper balance in the world's environment. A problem in one part of the world can have disastrous effects for other animals, even those living a long way away.

The Science Squad members looked at each other. They knew how important this was.

"When do we go?" Reggie asked excitedly.

"Your flight leaves in two hours," Professor Q answered. "I've booked you into a local hotel, and your GERA credit cards are loaded with enough money for living expenses and any emergencies that might happen. Jada has all the information on her tablet, and the rest of you have printouts. Study it on your flight. Oh, and good luck!"

The team had a long flight from Los Angeles to Taipei, and then a shorter flight on a tiny, shaky plane. When they landed, they had a long moonlit walk ahead of them before reaching the tiny Bamboo Inn on a small island between Taiwan and Japan.

"I hope we get posh rooms," said Cam hopefully.

Jada snorted with laughter. "Posh rooms, Cam?" she teased. "This inn only has four rooms, and we've got them all booked! I'll meet you all outside on the terrace in thirty minutes." She headed off to her room to shower and change, and then gathered her gear and headed out to the terrace.

Jada was the first one there. She sat down whilst
the owner of the inn brought fresh fish, vegetables and
fruit juice for the team. One by one the team emerged
from their rooms and sat down, ready to start working.

Soon munching could be heard across the terrace
as the squad members ate their delicious dinner.

"Okay, it's time to make a plan," Jada announced, putting down her knife and fork. She powered up her tablet and plugged in the satellite receiver, one of the gadgets given to her by Professor Q – after all, there was no way to get an internet connection on the island.

Cam flipped open his sleek laptop with the Science Squad logo on the cover. "I'm ready," he said.

"Let's start with what we know," Jada said.

Reggie pulled the paperwork from Professor Q out of his bag and looked at the report.

"There are a lot of sick porpoises swimming in these waters, which is unusual because the porpoise population has been healthy and stable over the last ten years," said Reggie.

"Which means something has changed to make the porpoises sick – some kind of change in their environment," Kate added.

Jada busily typed on her tablet. "So how do we find out what caused the change?"

Reggie twirled his pencil in his fingers. "Well, first we need to actually see the porpoises . . ."

Cam interrupted, "Someone down on the beach might have noticed something. Maybe we should head down there when it's light tomorrow morning and talk to people on the beach."

Kate looked up from the notes Professor Q had given them. "It says here that a Dr Vloodman reported the problem. There's a mobile phone number, and he has a little research station down by the beach. Let's go down and talk to him first thing in the morning."

Reggie nodded. "But for now, we should go to bed," he said. The team said good night to one another and headed back to their tiny rooms.

Chapter 2

The next morning, the team stood outside the front of the inn and looked around at the small town in daylight. There wasn't much to it: the small inn, some houses, and a few other guesthouses that served the tourists who came mainly to see the porpoises. There were hardly any people in sight, and the beach was a two-mile walk from the town.

Outside, in front of the inn, Reggie found a taxi to take them to the beach. But just as he opened the door, a man carrying a briefcase came from nowhere, rushed past him, and jumped in. Kate noticed the letters *DDJ* written on the man's briefcase, and a whiff of citrus and cedar floated out of the window behind him.

Reggie stood open-mouthed, watching the taxi speed off.

"That's rude!" muttered Cam, wrinkling his nose at the smell. He spotted four rickety old-fashioned bikes at the front of the hotel. Nodding to Reggie, he said, "We can use these bikes to get to the beach. That will solve our transportation problem."

After a bumpy, uncomfortable ride on the old bikes, they reached the beach and quickly found Dr Vloodman's research station. They gently pushed open the door to the small, weather-beaten hut. Dr Vloodman looked extremely relieved to see them. "You must be the Science Squad," he said. "Thank you for coming so quickly."

Stacks of papers cluttered his desk, and charts and coastal maps covered every inch of wall space in the tiny wooden hut.

Dr Vloodman smiled and peered at the team through thick lenses. "I am so grateful that Professor Q sent you. We have to find out what's wrong with our porpoises before it spreads. Also, they attract tourists, and as you'll have seen, the town is pretty quiet at the moment . . ."

"That's why we're here," Jada said. "Just tell us what you know."

"Well, about two weeks ago, we started getting reports from fishermen down on the beach about the porpoises acting peculiarly," he said.

"Can you describe their odd behaviour?" Reggie asked.

Dr Vloodman frowned. "Most of the fishermen on our island are very secretive," he began. "They don't like to talk to officials like me. You see, our town is so small that everyone knows everyone else. You might have better luck since you don't have an official look." He glanced at Reggie's shorts and scruffy trainers, and Kate's leggings.

"We like to be comfortable," said Cam, looking down at his clothes. "And anyway, we work outside, hacking our way through dense forest, wading through swamps, and climbing mountains."

Kate interrupted. "Have you seen any unusual algae in the water?" she asked.

"No, there's just what you would expect to find in these coastal waters," Dr Vloodman replied.

He talked for a few more minutes, but he didn't have any answers. It looked as if the survival of the porpoises was in the hands of the Science Squad. They thanked Dr Vloodman and promised to let him know what they found.

"Wait, one more thing," Dr Vloodman called just as the team was about to squeeze out of the tiny door. "The Coast Guard told me that a barge loaded with mining equipment drifted very close to our island a few weeks ago.

Apparently, the barge had broken down. It would have been a disaster if it had tipped and that oily equipment had landed in our waters. Anyway, the crew worked on the barge overnight, but by the next morning, it had vanished."

"The mysterious vanishing barge," Kate said. "When did this happen?"

"Ten days before I sent the first porpoise report to Professor Q," said Dr Vloodman.

"Okay. I'll need to know where the barge was when it broke down, its route here, and its final destination," said Kate as she opened a map app on her tablet and keyed in the information.

"Thank you, Dr Vloodman," Reggie said as he put his notes into his backpack. "We'll be sure to tell Professor Q how helpful you've been."

Chapter 3

Ten minutes later, while Reggie and Kate walked towards the ocean, Jada and Cam spotted a family returning from snorkelling.

As they took off their snorkelling equipment, Jada approached the family. "I bet you saw a lot of cool things down there," she said, smiling.

A little boy piped up, "Yeah, we saw the coral reefs! Did you know coral is a skeleton? We saw lots of skeletons."

"Who are you?" asked the boy's mother.

"We're scientists," said Jada. "We've come to study the porpoises."

The boy's sister's eyes widened on hearing about the porpoises.

"I saw something strange," she said, "really strange."

"What?" Jada and Cam asked at the same time. Jada pulled out her tablet.

"Two things, actually," said the girl. "Well, one was not so much seeing as *not* seeing . . . there weren't any fish on the coral reef. We didn't see *one*!"

Jada's ears pricked up.

The girl continued. "And then this porpoise swam right past us, and it looked hungry. It was really thin. I thought for a minute it might try to eat me!"

The children's mother looked at her daughter, alarmed. "You didn't tell me about this!" she said. Then she turned to Jada. "Is there something wrong with the porpoises? Could we be in danger?"

Jada smiled reassuringly. "No, I'm sure it's nothing serious – just stay away from them for now. I'm sure everything will be fine."

"And thanks," said Cam as he waved goodbye to the family. Jada and Cam jogged to meet up with Kate and Reggie. Cam quickly filled them in on what the two children had said.

Reggie looked out at the sparkling blue ocean. "How strange that there were no fish. None at all! That would certainly explain the porpoise being thin, but where have the fish gone?" He removed an empty glass bottle from his lab kit.

"What's that for?" Kate asked.

"I think we should analyse the water," Reggie said. "I have a feeling there's something in it that shouldn't be there, and it's driving the fish away."

"Is that what you're trying to prove by testing the water?" Cam asked.

"That's right," Reggie said as he filled the bottle with a sample of seawater. With a marker, he labelled it "Surface Beach Water" and added the date and time. He used a thermometer to measure its temperature, and then he also measured the air temperature. "I need another sample from deeper in the ocean, and then I'll compare the two," he said, recording everything in his notebook.

"I've got an idea. Reggie and I can rent a boat to get the deep water sample," said Kate, pointing to a sign on a building further down the beach that read 'Coral Reef Boats and Boards'. "You two can finish the interviews with the people on the beach – try talking to those fishermen over there."

"Okay, see you later," Cam said, as he and Jada walked toward the cluster of fishing boats and fishermen cleaning their catch.

"Hello," Jada began. "We're wondering what has been happening to the porpoises. A girl over there just told us the strangest story about a hungry porpoise."

"Well, now, I used to see quite a few," said one of the fishermen. "I take out my boat, *Lucky Duck*, at exactly 4:00 A.M. every Monday, Wednesday, and Friday, and I used to see four or five pods of porpoises. Maybe six or seven porpoises in each pod."

"So around 24 to 35 porpoises," Cam said.

"You're right. That's exactly what I used to see."
The man smiled at Cam.

Jada looked up from her notes and asked, "What about now?"

"Well, young lady, today I only saw one pod. Three porpoises were in that one. And I also saw two porpoises swimming alone – that's very unusual. They had an odd look in their eyes ... it was strange ..."

"So today you saw five porpoises – only five?" Cam was shocked.

"That's exactly what I saw." The fisherman shrugged.

Jada typed as fast as she could into her tablet. "And did you happen to notice any other odd behaviour?"

"Not that I remember," the fisherman continued. "But that barge that came out of nowhere dredged up such a mess that it scared all of our fish away. We didn't catch anything that day." The other fishermen grumbled in agreement. "It said 'DDJ' on the side of it, or at least I think that's what it said . . . it was hard to see," the fisherman continued.

"Thank you," Cam said. "Do you mind if we come back if we have other questions?"

"Anytime, anytime," said the fisherman.

"Well, that was interesting," said Jada, as they walked up the beach.

Cam nodded in agreement. "Let's get a snack and wait for the others to come back," he suggested. They went to a nearby café and sat down at a table. Jada started snapping pictures of the view as they waited for their food to arrive.

＊　＊　＊

Meanwhile, the little boat rocked in the current as Kate put on her diving gear and pulled a camera and some water sample bottles out of her backpack. Then she attached the underwater camera and a sample bottle to her diving belt, checked their location on her tablet, and compared it to the barge's location. They were on target.

"Okay, I'm ready," she told Reggie.

"Good luck, and be careful. I'll be here when you come up."

Kate saluted him, flipped backwards into the water, and disappeared into the depths. *It's beautiful down here,* she thought. She began snapping pictures and recording the temperature and her depth below the surface.

She got the water sample and recorded the temperature again. Looking down, she realised the water below her looked murky and muddy, and there were no fish. In fact, she was the only thing swimming around. It was strange that there weren't any fish in this part of the ocean – after all, it wasn't that far offshore. Kate dived deeper. She could just make out a structure that reminded her of playground equipment – a climbing frame and a slide. She took some more pictures but didn't expect to see anything because of the shadowy water. Then she slowly rose to the surface.

"That took you long enough,"
Reggie said when Kate's head
bobbed up from the ocean.

Kate glared at him through her mask.

"Thank you, Kate," Reggie said.

"That's more like it," Kate
said as she handed Reggie the water
sample, thermometer and camera.
Then she removed her diving gear.
"Let's go back to the hotel so you can
analyse this sample. I have a feeling it will be
totally different from the first sample. I bet our
deep seawater will have some answers. Also, I have
some pictures I want to look at."

Chapter 4

That evening, the Science Squad met in Jada's room
to report their findings. Cam and Jada filled in Kate
and Reggie on their conversations with the fishermen.
As they went through the part about the barge, Cam
mentioned the *DDJ* initials the fisherman had seen on
the side of the barge.

"DDJ . . . DDJ . . ." Kate muttered. "Where have I seen that before . . . wait!" The rest of the Science Squad turned to look at Kate. "I saw it this morning," she continued. "That rude man who stole our taxi – his briefcase said 'DDJ' on the side, I'm sure of it!"

Cam interrupted her, "And in the café on the beach I smelled that odd smell again, a sort of citrus and cedar smell . . . "

"You went to the café without us?" said Kate, disappointed.

"Hang on," said Jada. "What about those photos I took at the café? Maybe we should have a look at them. Cam, pass me your laptop."

Jada quickly uploaded the pictures and began flicking through them one by one, looking at them carefully. Suddenly she spotted something. "Look – there!" she cried to the rest of the team. The team peered over her shoulder, and there in the background of her photo was the man from the taxi holding his briefcase. Sure enough, it had the letters *DDJ* on the side of it.

Jada zoomed in and studied the man's picture closely. "I think I'll use my picture recognition software to find out who this man is," she said.

It only took a few minutes before Jada had a name. "His name, at least his current one, is Drake Darkly. He's well-known in the precious gems business, and not in a good way. He is wanted for scamming people out of their money through a company called Drake Darkly Jewels. He called himself a miner and sold worthless silver mines. He's believable because he has a degree in mining engineering," she said.

"Drake Darkly Jewels . . ." said Cam. "Hang on! DDJ!"

"That would make sense," said Reggie, "and the mining information fits with my water analysis. I found sediment from the seabed in water from near the surface of the sea, which would happen if someone had been mining nearby. That would certainly explain where all of the fish have gone."

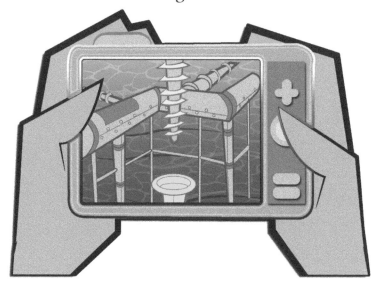

"And look at these pictures," Kate said, showing the team the pictures of the structure she'd seen while diving. "I know it's fuzzy, but it's from the area where the barge supposedly broke down. I bet that's mining equipment."

"Come to think of it, Cam and I heard an interesting story when we were at the café," Jada said.

"Interesting?" Cam said. "I think it was more like someone was pulling your leg."

"For years," Jada began, ignoring Cam, "a lady in the town told a story to anyone who would listen. It was about an underwater mine worth billions – not millions – *billions*. The mine was supposed to be full of precious opals, but she never had anything to show for it, not one single opal. Then she just disappeared."

The team listened carefully as Jada continued:
"And we also got a tip about bright lights on the
water, more recently, late at night. The café owner had
seen the lights a couple of times while he was locking
up for the night."

"Well, it sounds like we've got our guy," said Cam.
"Drake Darkly, illegal jewel miner and ocean polluter!
But what now?"

"Now we have to prove it," said Kate, gathering
her things.

Chapter 5

On the way out of the inn, Cam made a phone call to Dr Vloodman and told him that if Drake Darkly were involved in illegal underwater mining, he would be breaking enough laws and environmental regulations to get himself locked away for a long, long time. He was also facing a hefty fine. Cam told Dr Vloodman the Science Squad's plan, and Dr Vloodman promised to pass on the information to the local police.

The team rented the same boat as before, but this time they all went along. They sped along to their last location, and then they switched off the motor.

"Ready, Kate? Remember, we just need a few opal samples and pictures of mining activity," Reggie said. "Then when we get back to shore, the police will have all they need to arrest Darkly."

Wearing her diving equipment, Kate high-fived the team and jumped into the water. Seconds later, she disappeared below the surface. Kate checked her depth dial, swimming down slowly and gently so as not to alert anyone hiding in the mine. The Global Environmental Research Agency depended on her.

She focused until she reached the "playground." Close up, she saw it really was mining equipment. The enclosed slide led down into the mine, but it was small – barely large enough for her and her dive tank. *I bet there's another opening,* she thought. *But there's no time to look for it now.*

To reach the enclosed, tunnel-like slide, Kate had to hold onto the bars of what looked like a climbing frame and slowly, bar by bar, climb up to the entrance of the tunnel

She made it. *Stay calm*, she told herself. *Get the opal samples, take some pictures, and swim back to the boat and the rest of the squad.*

The tunnel led to an airlock, which Kate entered. The door locked behind her, and the water began to drain out. Once it had all drained away, a second door opened, and she found herself in a cave-like room, well-lit and filled with equipment. She snapped pictures of it and close-ups of serial and model numbers. A twinkling on the cave walls caught her eye—the opals! With her knife, Kate dug out a few of the sparkling gems and put them in a drawstring pouch.

Suddenly Kate saw movement to her right. A shadow emerged from the darkest corner of the mine, then a figure moved towards her – it was Drake Darkly! Hoping the tunnel was the fastest exit, Kate spun back the way she had come and somersaulted towards the tunnel. She heard grunts and running footsteps behind her, but her somersault was timed perfectly, and she landed at the airlock opening, head first.

Drake Darkly banged on the door, but it was already too late – the door had locked and the airlock chamber was filling with water as Kate took pictures of him standing in the mine.

As soon as the chamber was full of water, the second door opened, releasing Kate back into the ocean. Moving her flippers as fast as she could, she swam up as fast as she dared, which felt very slow.

Finally, she reached the surface, took off her mask, and yelled, "I've got it!" to the rest of the team, who were waiting in the boat.

* * *

The first thing the team noticed as they sped back to shore was Dr Vloodman and several uniformed officers. Once they got off the boat, Kate told the story of her underwater ordeal and held up her pouch of opal chips and the underwater camera. After seeing the evidence, Dr. Vloodman told the officers to arrest Drake Darkly as soon as he reached the mainland.

"If you don't need us, we're going to rest for the night," Jada said.

"You deserve much more than that," Dr Vloodman told them. "We'll talk later."

Out on the terrace the next morning, the team called Professor Q. "I've already talked to Vloody," she said.

"Vloody?" the team members mouthed silently to one another.

"And it is a good thing he called me, since my Science Squad decided sleep was more important than updating me."

"But Professor Q, Kate had a terrifying experience and we were so worried and . . ." Cam began.

"That was a joke, Cam," Professor Q said. "Surely you recognise a joke? Vloody will dismantle the mine. Once the sediment settles on the seabed, the water will return to acceptable levels. The porpoise population is safe, and so is our environment – for now. Take a week off. This is another triumph for GERA!" She hung up.

"A week off? Surf's up! Let's go!" said Reggie, but Kate was already out of the door.